Albert's Plot

A Play

Bob Hartwell

A SAMUEL FRENCH ACTING EDITION

SAMUEL FRENCH

FOUNDED 1830

SAMUELFRENCH-LONDON.CO.UK
SAMUELFRENCH.COM

CHARACTERS

Albert Briggs
Sally Parsons, his grand-daughter
Stanley Fothergill
Ms Charlesworth
Denis Parsons, Albert's son-in-law
Lottie Briggs, Albert's wife
Fiona Sinclair
Councillor Hamshaw

The scene is a street and allotment in a Northern town

Time—the present

Character Descriptions

Albert Briggs—late fifties, early sixties. Former miner, retired with respiratory disease, stubborn, forthright views on life.

Sally Parsons—late teens. Albert's grand-daughter, student at local polytechnic, cheerful and positive character.

Stanley Fothergill—late forties. Local newspaper reporter on his holiday, articulate, dreams of fame and fortune, but basically one of life's also-rans.

Ms Charlesworth—late thirties, early forties. An employee of the local council, abrupt manner, rather bitter.

Dennis Parsons—forties. Albert's son-in-law, a reasonable man but with limited horizons and imagination.

Lottie Briggs—late fifties, early sixties. Albert's wife, has a healthy respect for the system and authority, but more intelligent than she is given credit for.

Fiona Sinclair—early-mid 30's. Local parliamentary candidate for the Ecology Party, well bred, earnest.

Councillor Hamshaw—late fifties, early sixties. Labour mayor of the town, a self-made man who alternates between bullying and unsubtle persuasion to get his own way.

ALBERT'S PLOT

A street near to the centre of a Northern town. A morning on a fine day in autumn

On one side of the street is an allotment, the end of a row. The allotment is uneven and covered in grass and contains assorted rubbish—broken tools, seed boxes etc. Towards the rear is the front of a garden shed. Around the allotment is a wire fence which sags badly. On the fencing is a street sign which reads "Alamein Terrace cul-de-sac". Also fixed to this fencing is a typewritten Council notice. A gate in the fencing leads into the allotment where a folding garden chair is set up. On the other side of the street is a long park bench and a full waste paper bin

The set plan on page 35 shows an alternative in-the-round setting. It should be noted that the posts supporting the wire fence should be short to avoid blocking the audience's view whether an in-the-round or proscenium setting is used

As the Curtain *rises the stage is in darkness. A telephone rings and the voice of Councillor Hamshaw, the Mayor, is heard answering it*

Hamshaw (*off*) Mayor's parlour ... Yes, Hamshaw speaking ... Ah, Mr Simkins, you got my message ... No, no, I just wanted to check that everything was on schedule for the opening. I mean, it's less than a fortnight now ... The furniture and fittings are all done? Good, good. And the car park? ... Tarmac down already? Excellent ... Slight problem? What do you mean Mr Simkins, a slight problem? ... Well, solve it Mr Simkins, solve it. That's what slight problems exist for. For people like you to solve them ... *I* don't know who you should send. That's for you to decide. And quick ... What do you mean, flu epidemic? Listen Simkins, if you think the crowning glory of my year as Mayor is going to be ruined by a slight problem and a so-called flu epidemic in the planning department, then think again ... That's it, Simkins, send Ms Charlesworth down there to sort it out. If she's the one I think she is, she's the right man for the job.

I mean she scares the shit out of me, if you'll pardon my French
... And good morning to you, Mr Simkins.

*During the latter part of this conversation, the light gradually
increases to reveal Albert Briggs sitting in a garden chair on his
allotment. He is reading* The Daily Mirror, *smoking a foul-smelling
pipe, and he coughs frequently*

Sally enters

Sally Grandad, you've done it! I said you would.
Albert Of course I have. When I say I'm going to do something, I
  do it.
Sally I told them at home you would. They said it was all talk.
  Then Mum started slagging you off ...
Albert As usual.
Sally ... as usual. And Dad said we had to make allowances.
Albert Make allowances? Why is it that your father can make
  perfectly ordinary English sound like a dreadful insult? And
  what did you say, Sally? Were you on my side?
Sally Oh yes, Grandad, I'm on your side.
Albert I knew I could rely on you. You know what's right and
  what's wrong.
Sally Well, it's not just that. I had a five pound bet with Dad that
  you'd see it through.
Albert Typical of the younger generation! Why are they only
  interested in money?
Sally In my case, probably because I've never got any.
Albert Did you get the paper?
Sally Yes, it's here.
Albert Is the notice in again?
Sally Yes, same as last week. (*She goes round to check the Council
  notice on the wire fence*) Just the same wording as this one.
Albert They haven't changed their minds then.
Sally Did you honestly think they would?
Albert No, I suppose not. I did hope there might be a sudden
  outbreak of common sense at the borough council, but I
  suppose that's too much to expect.
Sally Oh I nearly forgot. I brought you a flask of tea.
Albert You're a good girl, Sally.
Sally Don't gulp it down too fast. I put a little something in it.

Albert Not Dennis's ten-year-old malt whisky. You'll be in trouble my girl. He marks the level with a pencil you know. (*He unscrews the flask and pours*)

Sally Don't worry, there's the same amount left in the bottle. It's just not quite as strong as it was.

Albert I don't know where you get your cunning from.

Sally I do.

Albert (*drinking*) Oh that's beautiful. With tea like that a man could take on the world.

Sally I think you may have to.

Albert What's happening at your house this morning?

Sally Oh, Mum was just thinking about getting up, and Dad was about to set off to do dynamic things in the retail trade.

Albert I see. Oh well, it's nice to know that my protest has caused such a stir down in Hazlewood Gardens. Was your grandma there?

Sally She arrived just as I left.

Albert How did she look?

Sally Worried.

Albert That's nothing new. Your grandma has this awful respect for officials and authority. I've tried telling her that authority is only there so that we've got something to moan about and argue with, but she'll never change.

Sally Mum and Dad are the same. Mum likes to think she can have her little protest, but only as long as it's respectable—her "good causes" as she calls them—and Dad actually believes that politicians are kind, generous, sincere, human beings.

Albert But we know different, don't we love?

Sally Do you know, we could do with you at the Poly. Shake up the trainee accountants and electrical engineers a bit.

Albert No, I don't think I could cope with all that essay writing.

Sally Nor can I, most of the time. Here, don't tell Mum and Dad I said that. They think I should be hard-working, clean-living and eternally grateful to society.

Albert The only thing you need to be grateful for, love, is that you've got the brains and you've used them. Don't let them brainwash you into being grateful to society. I mean what's society done for me? Taken away my health, taken away my job, and now bugger me if it doesn't want to take away my allotment. I mean, is that what I fought six years in the war for?

To let some piddling little civil servants take things away from me?

Sally Well, you didn't actually fight, Grandad, did you? That's a slight exaggeration.

Albert Listen, madam, when you get to my age, slight exaggerations are about the only excitement left to you. That and getting in the way of the powers-that-be.

Sally Oh, that reminds me. I've got a present for you. (*She rummages in her bag and takes out a large Union Jack which she unfolds*) I thought it might look good on the shed.

Albert Hey, that's smashing Sally. Where'd you get it from?

Sally I pinched it while I was on a Rock Against Racism march down in London last summer. This National Front gorilla was waving it about and shouting his mouth off. I could put up with that, but then he started casting doubts on my femininity.

Albert So what did you do?

Sally I cast doubts on his manhood.

Albert How?

Sally I kneed him in the nuts. And while he was groping around checking that his equipment was all there and still in the right place, I made off with his Union Jack.

Albert Do you know, it will always be one of life's great mysteries to me how two first class dillies like my daughter and son-in-law managed to produce a smashing kid like you. I reckon there must have been a mix-up at that maternity hospital.

Sally Come on, let's get this flag up before you start to embarrass me.

They begin to put up the Union Jack on the front of the shed

Stanley Fothergill enters. He looks slightly seedy, and holds a carrier bag. He sits on the bench

Stanley 'Morning.

Albert and Sally turn and stare at the newcomer

Albert I beg your pardon?

Stanley (*slightly nonplussed*) I said "Morning".

Albert Yes, that's what I thought you said. (*To Sally*) Be careful, he could be from the council.

Sally moves to the edge of the allotment and stares at Stanley

Sally (*moving back to Albert*) He doesn't look as if he's from the council.

Albert Don't be fooled. I wouldn't put it past those buggers to send someone disguised as a human being.

Sally So what do we do?

Albert Ignore him. He might go away.

They continue to put up the flag

Stanley What are you doing?

Albert What does it look like we're doing?

Stanley Well, it looks like you're fixing a Union Jack to a garden shed.

Albert Then that's what we're doing.

Stanley Oh, I see.

They carry on

Some sort of celebration is it?

Sally You could say that.

Stanley Oh, I see. (*He roots around in his jacket pocket and takes out a diary. He opens it and reads*) October the sixteenth. British International Motor Show N.E.C. Birmingham: Oscar Wilde born eighteen fifty-four: First ever parachute jump made eighteen-oh-two. (*He puts the diary away*) Nothing there to get wildly excited about. Anyway, nice day for it.

Albert Nice day for what?

Stanley (*again thrown by Albert's remark*) Well, er ... nice day for fixing a Union Jack to a garden shed.

Albert Yes, well it would be if we didn't keep getting interrupted.

Sally Haven't you got a bus to catch or a dog to take for a walk?

Stanley No.

Sally Oh.

Stanley No, I've absolutely nothing to do but watch humanity going about its rightful, if rather mysterious, business.

Albert You what?

Stanley I am on holiday. Nothing to do and a whole two weeks to do it in. Well, five days actually. This is the second week.

Albert I didn't know we were on the tourist route.

Stanley We're not. Like you, I have the doubtful privilege of living here.

Sally (*to Albert*) Well at least we know he's not from the council.

Albert (*to Sally*) Do we though? We only know he's on holiday, but we don't know what he's on holiday *from*. It could still be a trap. I wouldn't put anything past that lot. (*To Stanley, with an air of casual interest*) Er . . . how are things at the council offices?

Sally (*under her breath*) Subtle, Grandad, very subtle.

Stanley I beg your pardon.

Albert How are things at the council offices?

Stanley Pretty reasonable, I should imagine. I mean if there's any sense of order in the universe, things at the council offices should be considerably better than at the crematorium, and somewhat worse than at the country club. Mind you, I'm not an expert. I only go there twice a year to pay·my rates.

Sally What he's trying to say is, are you a council official?

Stanley Why should I be a council official? I admit there have been times in my life when I've thought it might be an advantage to be someone else, but never in my wildest flights of fancy have I seen myself as a council official.

Sally Well that's got that sorted out at least.

Stanley For you maybe, but certainly not for me.

Sally Oh look, I'm sorry. This must seem very confusing. The thing is, the Council are trying to throw him off his allotment.

Stanley (*to Albert*) And you don't want to go?

Albert There's no *want* about it. I'm not going.

Stanley Very wise. As a general rule, I've always found that whenever anybody official wants you to do something, the safest thing is to do the opposite.

Sally There you are, he's on your side.

Albert I'd like to know who he is before I agree that he's on my side.

Stanley Oh I'm sorry. I haven't introduced myself. My name's Fothergill, Stanley Fothergill. Journalist, newspaper reporter, hack, man of words. Though I have to admit that most of them are mundane, instantly forgettable, and I regret to say often incorrectly spelt.

Sally A journalist. With you here they wouldn't dare to do anything. They couldn't take the publicity.

Stanley Oh, I wish I had your faith.

Albert Which paper are you with? *Express? Mirror? Yorkshire Post?*

Stanley A bit more humble and a lot nearer home. *The Chronicle.*

Albert The local paper? But it never covers anything but weddings and funerals. And then it gets the names wrong. That's not you is it?

Stanley I'm afraid so. My typing's not very accurate, and the type-setter has problems with his contact lenses.

Albert (*to Sally*) It's a bloody awful paper. You've often said so yourself.

Stanley It gets very embarrassing at times, I must admit. Last month I did a funeral in the morning and a wedding at noon. When we printed it, we'd got a nineteen year old virginal bride getting married to a man of eighty three who'd been dead for four days. Neither family was exactly overjoyed.

Sally But that doesn't matter. Just the threat of publicity will be enough. You will stay won't you? Just to back us up. And who knows, you might even get the story of a lifetime. (*She begins to exit*)

Albert Where are you going?

Sally Just down to the end of the road to check on enemy movement. Be back soon.

Sally exits

Stanley The story of a lifetime. I can just see it now. Front page of every national daily, "Lone Pensioner In Allotment Stake-Out Drama", by Stanley Fothergill. Yes, that's it. Fothergill of Fleet Street.

Albert Do you think they'd print it?

Stanley Put it like this. If you were to grow half a dozen rows of opium poppies on your allotment, then invite a troupe of topless go-go dancers to an orgy in which indescribable things were done with brussel sprouts and bean poles, you'd have a better than even chance. Otherwise, no.

Albert I thought not.

Stanley Pity though. Somewhere deep in my bones, I feel that there's a story just waiting for me to stumble across it. But it won't happen in this town, not now.

Albert What do you mean, not now?

Stanley I've got a theory ...

Albert I thought you might have.

Stanley I've got a theory that the vast majority of places are boring, dead-and-alive spots on the map where nothing ever happens. Take out London and a few other cities and what have you got left? A load of places that are nothing more than names on motorway exit signs. Pontefract, Kettering, Oswestry, Cleethorpes. But then one morning, a little old lady in Cleethorpes goes out to empty her tea leaves on her hydrangea, and there, underneath the plant, is a dismembered human body. She screams, faints, and for a few days the eyes of the nation are fixed on her little bit of the world. And then it's gone, moved on to somewhere else. A drugs ring uncovered in Bishop Auckland. Satanic rites in a cemetery in Yeovil and so on and so on. And it's never the same place twice. Or virtually never.

Albert I suppose this *is* leading somewhere?

Stanley Look at this town. A classic contender for the most boring town in Britain. I'd vote for it. But then suddenly a gang of vicious criminals hijack a Securicor van full of crisp new ten pound notes, and get away with a cool two hundred thousand pounds. And while the local constabulary are still sharpening their pencils and trying to remember how to use a fingerprint kit, the vicar of St. Botolph-on-the-Moor ups and runs off with his housekeeper, who just happens to be a buxom twenty-four-year-old au pair from Gothenburg.

Albert I think I remember reading about that.

Stanley Of course you do. Both those stories broke last week. Last week! Here! In this town! And where was Stanley Fothergill last week? On bloody holiday! Feeding half a dozen geriatric pigeons in the town hall square. Both those stories were covered by a nineteen-year-old cub reporter who's still breaking in his first Bic disposable razor. And now he's made it! He doesn't know one end of a biro from the other and he's on his way to Fleet Street.

Albert That's bad luck, I'll grant you that.

Stanley It's more than bad luck, it's a bloody disaster. I mean, that Securicor van makes that same journey every week without fail. Why did they have to choose last week? And that vicar. You'd have thought that out of Christian charity he could have wrestled with his conscience for another fortnight before running off with Inga the pneumatic Swede. Ah well, it's happened now. No more excitement for another fifty years at least.

Albert Unless this somehow develops into your big story.

Stanley Can't see it myself. I mean, I'll go through the motions for you. Frighten a few people. But the angles just aren't there. You get a nose for this sort of thing, even after years of covering weddings and funerals.

Albert Mind you, as Sally said, the threat of publicity might be enough.

Stanley I take it you and the young lady are related?

Albert What do you mean? She's my grand-daughter.

Stanley Pity. We might have had a re-run of the vicar and the au pair. Now that could have been an angle.

Albert You know, for a decent bloke, you've got a very nasty mind.

Stanley It's not my mind, it's just the way of the world. You'd be amazed at the number of old men who take their so-called nieces for candle-lit dinners and weekends at quiet hotels in the country. I once followed this Tory M.P. and a delightful young thing half way across Yorkshire. I was convinced it was front page stuff. Finally cornered them on the top floor of a smart hotel in Harrogate. I was just about to dot the "I's" and cross the "T's" when they came out of separate rooms with birth certificates blazing. Father and daughter, family resemblance there for all to see. Very nearly cost me my job.

Albert Well, Sally is my grand-daughter so there's no story there.

Stanley She seems a bright girl.

Albert Oh, she is. She's at the local polytechnic.

Stanley Really? What's she studying?

Albert Now she did tell me. Arc something. Arc welding I think it is.

Stanley They certainly study some strange things these days. Whatever happened to French and Geography and stuff like that?

Albert Archaeology, that's it.

Stanley She'd be better off with Arc Welding. You don't see many jobs for archaeologists in Situations Vacant.

Albert No but it comes in handy when I want the allotment dug. Just tell her there's a Roman lavatory under this lot and her and her cronies are swarming all over it. Clears the weeds a treat.

Stanley She seems to know her own mind.

Albert Oh yes, quite an independent girl is our Sally. Bit head-strong at times but then so she should be. Goes on these demonstrations you know. Sitting down in front of the police

cars. All over the road. Still it's better than doing nothing all day
like some of them. It keeps her off the streets.
Stanley Well, not exactly.
Albert Eh? Oh, I see what you mean. (*He starts to laugh at his own
mistake and has a coughing fit*)
Stanley Are you all right?

Sally enters

Sally Come on, Grandad, don't die on us yet. I think we've got
company. There's a woman marching this way with a very
severe look and a clipboard.
Albert A very severe look *and* a clipboard. That definitely sounds
official. Get ready Mr Fothergill. You might get your story yet.
Stanley I think I'll keep a low profile. Don't want to frighten her
off too soon. (*He takes out a newspaper from his carrier bag and
starts to read*)

*Ms Charlesworth enters. She stands for a moment surveying the
scene before her*

Ms Charlesworth (*to the street in general*) Mr Briggs?
Albert Who wants to know?
Ms Charlesworth Ah, Mr Briggs. Are you planning on staying
long?
Stanley (*quietly*) She makes it sound like a boarding house in
Morecambe.
Ms Charlesworth And who might you be?
Stanley Just an ordinary ratepayer enjoying the peace and tran-
quility of this crisp autumnal morning.
Ms Charlesworth Well, kindly go and enjoy it somewhere else.
Some of us have work to do.
Stanley Oh, don't mind me. I've never been one to stop other
people working.
Ms Charlesworth (*turning to Albert*) Now, Mr Briggs. I repeat my
question. How long do you plan to pursue this futile action of
yours?
Albert If you mean how long am I planning to stay here on my
own allotment, then the answer is as long as it takes for your lot
to change their minds.
Ms Charlesworth You seem to be somewhat confused, Mr Briggs.
The piece of land you are occupying is no longer an allotment. It

ceased to be an allotment last Friday at twelve noon, under the Zoned Land Allotments Act of nineteen-oh-six, Section four Subsection C. So how long can you possibly organise a protest over something which has quite simply ceased to exist?

Albert This allotment doesn't exist?

Ms Charlesworth Correct.

Albert So if I pick up a bloody great clod of this earth now and sling it at your head, you won't feel a thing?

Ms Charlesworth Are you threatening me, Mr Briggs?

Albert How can I threaten you with something that doesn't exist?

Ms Charlesworth That is an absurd argument. Totally absurd.

Sally Of course it is, Grandad. The lady's right. If the allotment doesn't exist and you're standing on the allotment, then you don't exist either.

Stanley There you are, your problem's solved. He doesn't exist.

Ms Charlesworth But of course he exists!

Stanley Well, that's easily remedied. Pass another law. If you can do it with allotments you can do it with people. I mean that land he's standing on looks like an allotment, he thinks it's an allotment, but it's not an allotment because the law says it's not. Likewise, he looks like a bloody-minded old man, you think he's a bloody-minded old man, but if you use those wonderful laws of yours he could cease to be a bloody-minded old man any time you choose.

Ms Charlesworth Mr Briggs, if we could bring this discussion back into the realms of reality.

Albert You started it, Missus.

Ms Charlesworth It's Ms, not Mrs. Ms Charlesworth.

Albert Are you really a Ms? Do you know, I've never met a Ms. I mean I've read about them in the papers but I never thought I'd meet one face to face. What's it like then, actually being a Ms?

Ms Charlesworth Mr Briggs, even if you refuse to accept the legal status of this piece of land, you cannot deny that it is owned by the council. Therefore as a duly appointed official of that council, it is my duty to inform you that you are trespassing. *And* that if you refuse to leave of your own free will, I will have you ejected with all possible speed and any necessary force.

Albert Now who's doing the threatening?

Stanley (*writing in his notebook*) "Bureaucrat Threatens Defence-less Ratepayer".

Ms Charlesworth What do you think you're doing?

Albert Mr Fothergill is a reporter. One of the best there is.

Sally Yes. I should be very careful what you say in front of Mr Fothergill.

Ms Charlesworth Fothergill? Aren't you the man who does weddings and funerals for *The Chronicle*?

Sally There you are Mr Fothergill. Your reputation is spreading.

Ms Charlesworth You reported the funeral of my late father. You spelt his name wrongly.

Albert (*quietly; to Sally*) Well, that didn't work, did it?

Sally Excuse me, Ms. Charlesworth. You just said that my grandfather, Mr Briggs, was trespassing.

Ms Charlesworth He is indeed.

Sally But how can he be trespassing when he's paid his allotment rental up until next August?

Albert (*quietly*) Shut up, Sally. I haven't even paid for last year, let alone next.

Ms Charlesworth I fear you are wrong, young lady. No allotment rentals have been accepted on the Alamein Terrace site for the coming year.

Sally Oh yes, they have. His.

Ms Charlesworth I repeat that no payments have been accepted. However, if you persist with this erroneous idea, I will prove to you that you are wrong. (*She flicks through pages on her clipboard*) Here we are. The figures on allotment receipts for the past three months. Which show quite clearly that . . . Oh.

Sally Quite clearly that what, Ms. Charlesworth?

Ms Charlesworth It is obviously a computer error.

Sally (*taking out a cheque book*) And this cheque stub? Is this a computer error too? You see, I paid the cheque in myself. Give me ten minutes and I can even fetch you the receipt.

Sally exits

Ms Charlesworth Oh dear, there has obviously been a breakdown in the Council's internal communication system. But no matter. I can issue you with an immediate refund.

Albert I don't want an immediate refund. I just want my allotment.

Ms Charlesworth You have to have a refund. (*She takes money out*

out of a plastic bank bag and approaches Albert) Here, take it.
(*She offers two five-pound notes*)
Albert No. (*He backs away from the money*)
Ms Charlesworth Very well. (*She very deliberately drops the notes over the fence on to the allotment*) There. One refund delivered.
Albert Do you honestly think this has anything to do with money? Here, I'll show you what I think of your so-called refund. (*He very carefully tears up the notes and drops the pieces on the pavement side of the fence*)
Ms Charlesworth You realize that dropping litter is an offence punishable by a fine of two hundred pounds?
Stanley (*getting up*) Ms. Charlesworth is right. We mustn't spoil the streets of our fair town with unsightly litter. (*He picks up all the pieces of the bank notes and carefully puts them in the waste bin*) All clean and tidy again, Ms. Charlesworth. (*He sits on the bench again*)
Ms Charlesworth Mr Briggs, I am a very busy woman. It might help us to resolve our problem if you were to tell me *why* you refuse to move from this allotment.
Albert I explained that in my letter.
Ms Charlesworth Ah yes, your letter. I'm afraid I haven't got it with me, but I think I can remember the main points. Six years valiant war service, forty years slaving underground to keep the wheels of industry turning, and now in the twilight of your years, a lone campaigner for the individual against the jack boot of local government dictatorship. The only thing missing from that letter was the tear-jerking violins in the background.
Albert I got your letter too. The Council's letter. The only thing missing from that was the English.
Ms Charlesworth I beg your pardon?
Albert Well, it was full of "herewiths" and "wheretofors", and parties of the first part and parties of the second part. It just didn't mean anything.
Ms Charlesworth Well, Mr Briggs, let me explain it to you in words that *will* mean something. We have closed your allotment, and the other allotments adjoining—(*she checks herself*)—next to yours because we need to build a road.
Albert Ah yes, but what sort of a road?
Ms Charlesworth Surely Mr Briggs a road is a road. The sort of road is immaterial.

Albert You see there's all sorts of roads. There's roads that lead sick people into hospitals, or take little kids to the seaside, or bring barrels of best bitter from the brewery. But your road isn't that sort of road, is it Ms. Charlesworth?

Ms Charlesworth No, it is not. It is quite simply a road into the car park of the new council offices.

Albert Ah no, it isn't. You see, I've looked at the plans. My grand-daughter and I exercised our democratic rights and went down to the council and we've seen the plans. It isn't a road *into* the car park, it's a road *out*. An exit road.

Ms Charlesworth And that makes a fundamental difference?

Albert Of course it does. One road takes people into work and the other takes them out. Now, I'd give up my allotment if you were going to build a hospital or a nursery school or a betting shop. I'd even consider it if you needed the land for a road *into* the council offices. But to give up all this so that a few dozen civil servants can get out of work quicker—no chance.

Stanley (*writing*) "Allotment Protest Hero Slams Lazy Civil Servants".

Ms Charlesworth Shut up, Mr Fothergill.

Stanley I see. Trying to gag the press now are we?

Ms Charlesworth You said "all this" Mr Briggs. What did you mean by "all this"?

Albert All this. My allotment.

Ms Charlesworth But Mr Briggs, your allotment is a total mess, an eyesore. There's nothing growing on it.

Albert This is fallow land, Ms. Charlesworth. Land is like people. Every so often you have to let land have a rest, build up its strength, recharge its batteries. Every good gardener knows that, though I wouldn't expect you to understand.

Ms Charlesworth For many years Mr Briggs, I had the misfortune to look after my father, an aged, infirm and singularly cantankerous old man who took away most of my useful life and gave me precious little in return. He had a garden, a very large garden in which he took great pride. He had the pride, Mr Briggs, but I had the daily drudgery of battling with that garden. I dug it, manured it, weeded it, planted it, harvested it. Of course it was his name on the prize certificates at the garden produce show, even though it was my sweat that produced it all. Don't talk to me about land, Mr Briggs, I'm an expert. I've forgotten more about brassicas and root crops than you'll ever know. And when at last I buried him, I sold the house and bought a flat with not so much as a single window box. And the one consolation I had was that I would never look upon his like again. But I was wrong, wasn't I, Mr Briggs? Well, I'm warning you, I'm leaving now but I shall be back to have you removed by legitimate means or otherwise. And you can write *that* in your little note-book, Mr Fothergill. But I should check the spelling of legiti-mate. It's probably not a word you're familiar with.

Ms Charlesworth exits

Albert sits in his chair

Albert What a woman!

Stanley Awful wasn't she? A real dragon!

Albert Marvellous woman! Imagine having a marital bust-up with a woman like that. You'd know you'd been in an argument. Have to keep ducking and weaving to survive more than five minutes with her. And she can dig gardens.

Stanley Do you know, when she said she buried her father, I almost believed she'd dug the grave herself.

Albert She probably did. What a woman!

Sally enters

Sally What are you looking so happy about? I've just rushed back here, thinking I'd have to go round with a wheelbarrow picking up the pieces, and you sit there with a daft look on your face.

Stanley I think he's in love.

Sally Him? He doesn't know the meaning of the word. I think the only time I've ever seen him show true affection is when he's got his hand grasped warmly round a pint of beer.

Albert No, but you've got to admit, Stanley Fothergill, that she's a formidable woman.

Stanley Oh, yes, I'll admit that. Totally formidable.

Sally I assume that the object of his undying passion is our Ms. Charlesworth. Where's she gone, by the way?

Stanley I think she mentioned something about invading Poland.

Sally Do you reckon she'll come back?

Albert Oh yes, she'll come back. I think I'd be disappointed if she didn't. She'll have gone to lick her wounds and then she'll attack again.

Stanley You were very impressive, Mr Briggs.

Albert Call me Albert. All this Mr Briggs stuff makes me nervous.

Stanley The bit that really impressed me was the bit with the money.

Sally (*suspiciously*) What bit with what money?

Albert Ah well, you see Sally . . .

Stanley Our Ms Charlesworth offered your Grandad ten pounds for the allotment refund and he very quietly, and with great dignity, I thought, tore it up and dropped the pieces at her feet. It was a lovely moment.

Sally I'm sure it was. It's easy to behave with great dignity when it's not your own money you're tearing up.

Albert But I had to do it Sally. I couldn't take that money. It was a matter of principle. Surely you can see that.

Sally I suppose so.

Albert Except that I can't help feeling that when this is all over, tearing up that money is the one bit I'll look back on with regret.

Stanley (*getting up and moving to the waste bin*) Come on now, Albert, we can't have our lone fighter for individual liberty weighed down with feelings of regret. (*He carefully takes the pieces of notes from the bin*) Here you are. Excuse the baked bean juice. All you need now is a ton and a half of sellotape and they'll be as good as new.

Albert Stanley Fothergill, you're a genius.

Stanley No, just careful where money's concerned.

Albert Do you know, this is turning out to be quite a day.

Sally Well, I'm sorry to ruin your happiness, but I think those are mine.

Albert Oh Sally, you wouldn't.

Sally Oh yes, I would. (*She takes the pieces and carefully places an old seed tray upside down near the allotment, sits and begins to reassemble the money*)

Dennis Parsons and Lottie Briggs enter

Dennis Sally, get away from that allotment and come home this instant.

Sally I can't, I'm busy making money.

Albert and Stanley find this very funny and laugh uproariously. Albert's laugh disintegrates into a cough

Dennis Well, I don't know what everyone finds so amusing. Now will you come home, Sally? Or do I have to resort to force?

Sally Oh come off it, Dad, it's a bit late to play the macho man in public. I mean, if you want to try that sort of thing you should have started years ago before Mum pinched all the trousers. Besides, I should be careful if I were you. The press are here.

Dennis What? Where?

Albert That gentleman over there is Fearless Fothergill, the scourge of Fleet Street.

Lottie Does that mean we'll be in the papers? Oh I do hope not. Printed there for all to see with all those common criminals and sex maniacs.

Stanley Now don't worry, madam. Assuming that this gentleman (*indicating Dennis*) keeps his violent emotions in check, you have nothing to fear.

Dennis But what are you doing here?

Stanley Now don't you worry Mr … er …

Dennis Parsons. Dennis Parsons.

Sally Oh that was a mistake, Dad, giving your name to a reporter.

Dennis What? Oh yes. Forget I said that.

Sally Don't whatever you do tell him that you live at twenty-one Hazlewood Gardens.

Dennis Sally! Kindly shut up!

Sally I'm an adult now, Father. I have the right to free speech. This is England, you know.

Dennis Yes, but it won't be for long with disruptive elements like him chipping away at the whole democratic process.

Albert Isn't it amazing? When I got up this morning I was just an old man with an allotment. Now I'm a threat to the state.

Dennis (*to Stanley*) Now listen Mr …

Stanley Fothergill, but you can call me Stanley.

Dennis Now listen Mr Fothergill, I don't know what you are doing here, but I trust I can rely on your discretion.

Sally Dad, he's a reporter. If reporters relied on discretion, every newspaper in the country would go out of business tomorrow.

Stanley Do not worry, Mr Parsons, I am at present on holiday. I shall merely sit here enjoying the view. Of course, I may listen from time to time, but that is an instinctive reaction for a journalist.

Dennis Only this is a very delicate time for me.

Albert God, he makes it sound like a bride on her wedding night.
Sally If you're going to talk about your promotion again Dad, I think I *will* go home.
Lottie Don't be horrible Sally. This promotion is very important to your father.
Sally Yes but does it have to be important to all of us?
Albert All the time?
Dennis Look, all I'm trying to do is better myself. Join the management. Why that should be treated with such scorn I do not know.
Sally Oh Dad, stop being so pompous.
Lottie Sally, will you stop being so rude to your poor father. I blame you for this, Albert.
Albert I thought you might.
Sally I mean, what are we talking about? What is all this "join the management" rubbish? You are hoping, praying, begging to be made Head of Dairy Products at a prehistoric family super-market.
Dennis Dairy Products *and* Cooked Meats, Sally. It will give me the chance to diversify.
Lottie And there's more money, Sally. Your father needs the money with you at that college. You mustn't forget that.
Sally I'm never allowed to forget it.
Dennis You see now, Mr Fothergill, why any adverse publicity would be disastrous at this stage. Brownlow and Williamson are a very traditional firm. They adopt a high moral stance on staff appointments. I mean, Eric Golder was in with a very reasonable chance of getting Wines and Spirits last year, until they found something dubious in his private life.
Albert What was that?
Dennis I believe he was living with a married woman.
Lottie Don't listen to this, Sally.
Sally No Grandma.
Dennis Of course it was never actually stated. These things never are. But he'll be a counter assistant now for the rest of his days. Well that's not going to happen to me. I deserve this chance. I've already proved myself in Dairy Products and I know I can do things with Cooked Meats.
Stanley All this talk of food is too much for me. (*He roots through*

his carrier bag, takes out a packet of sandwiches, sits down and begins to eat)

Dennis (*to Albert*) That is why you've got to stop this silly protest of yours before you ruin my chances. You've already thrown my schedule out for the day. I'm supposed to be at a Lymeswold tasting in Huddersfield at two o'clock.

Albert And if I won't stop?

Dennis Then I'm afraid I won't be responsible for my actions.

Stanley Oh dear. This is getting serious. "Dairy Products Executive In Vicious Attack". Now where's my notebook?

Sally Be careful Father. He obviously feels a front page story coming on.

Lottie Oh Dennis, do watch what you're saying. Remember that Eric person.

Dennis Don't worry, mother-in-law. I can handle this. I haven't worked in the retail trade for twenty-six years without learning a thing or two about human nature. (*He approaches Stanley*) Ah, lunchtime I see, Mr Fothergill. And what little delicacies have we got in our sandwiches today?

Stanley Just cheese.

Dennis Cheese? And what sort of cheese?

Stanley I don't know. One cheese is very much like another.

Dennis Now that's where you're wrong. May I? (*He takes Stanley's sandwich, extracts a morsel of cheese and delicately nibbles it*) Ah yes, that is Tesco's Double Gloucester at one pound twenty-nine a pound. A nice enough little cheese in its own way but perhaps a little bland. Now I'd have thought you were a Stilton man. Yes, a whole Stilton, slow matured, sealed in wax the proper way you know, and stored at marginally below room temperature.

Stanley Seems a lot of trouble to go to over a piece of cheese.

Dennis But it's worth it Mr Fothergill. I'll get you one and you'll see what I mean. Now, what's in the other packet of sandwiches?

Stanley Meat paste.

Dennis Meat paste? You cannot be serious Mr Fothergill. I can see I'll have to introduce you to the joys of duck liver paté. We at Brownlow and Williamson do a particularly fine one, in its own earthenware bowl. Retails at four pounds, ninety-five but of course we don't need to worry about that. You can take it as a token of my gratitude.

Stanley Take it where?

Dennis Anywhere you like, as long as its away from Alamein Terrace.

Stanley Thanks for the offer Mr Parsons, but I think I'll stay. Compared to the rich human activity on show here today, your Stilton and your duck liver paté sound just a little . . . what was the word you used . . . bland.

Albert Thank you, Stanley. Good try Dennis, but you'll have to do better than that.

Dennis Okay, father-in-law, so you won't listen to me. My career means nothing to you. Perhaps I was a fool to think that it ever would. But at least listen to your own wife.

Lottie Pardon?

Dennis Tell him mother-in-law.

Lottie Tell him what?

Dennis What we were discussing on the way over here.

Sally You mean what you told her to say.

Lottie No, he didn't, Sally. That's where you're wrong. You think that because I'm married to a man who won't let me get a word in edgeways, that I've got nothing to say. But I have.

Albert Well then love, get on and say it.

Lottie You know what I've got to say. I've said it often enough in the last eighteen months.

Albert Oh not that old folks' home nonsense again. Do you know, you and Dennis are like a couple of records with the needle stuck. Him going on about his promotion and you forever nattering on about us going to an old people's home.

Lottie It's not an old people's home, it's a warden assisted flat.

Albert Same difference. Just because they change the name doesn't mean it'd be any different. They stuck Billy Rawson from the end of the road in one a few years back. It was terrible. I only went to see him once. Couldn't stand to go again. Matron with eyes like a hawk. And a beak to match. Just waiting to pounce if he didn't eat all his semolina pudding.

Lottie But you cook your own food in a warden assisted flat.

Albert We cook our own food now, so what's the point of moving from our own home. We've been in that home now for forty years.

Lottie Yes, and look at it. It's like us Albert. It's seen better days.
Albert You speak for yourself.
Lottie I'm trying to, but you won't listen.
Albert Lovely little house. Moved in as soon as we got married.
Lottie Yes, love, it was lovely then. When we were younger. But not any more. The roof needs doing and the windows let in the wind and the rain, and every bit of traffic seems to make it shake. And it's not doing your health any good staying there.
Albert I'll be all right. You've never heard me complain.
Lottie No, but I'll tell you what I have heard. I've heard you coughing on a night. I've heard your breath rattling in your chest trying to fight its way in and out. I've even heard you shivering, yes *heard* you, because you're too cold to get to sleep.
Albert Don't worry about me. I can stand it.
Lottie Why do you have to be so stubborn? It's not brave or clever to put up with things when there's something better just waiting for you to put out your hand and take it. That's not brave. It's stupid.
Albert I still don't see why I should just up and walk out of my own home.
Lottie Because if you don't walk out soon, they'll be carrying you out. In a wooden box. And then I'll be expected to weep for you. Well, I could weep for you now, you stupid old man.

There is a moment's embarrassed silence. Stanley breaks it

Stanley What's it like, Mrs Briggs, this home with the warden assisted flats?
Lottie Oh, it's lovely Mr Fothergill. I've got a leaflet here that they gave me when I went to have a look. I had to go on my own of course. He wouldn't come with me. (*She takes a leaflet out of her bag, gives it to Stanley, and sits down on the bench beside him*) It's got double glazing *and* central heating. And you've got your own front door with your own key. And there's an electric bell on the wall in the kitchen in case you need help. And they organise entertainment as well.
Albert Yes, Bingo five nights a week whether you like it or not.
Stanley It looks very nice Mrs Briggs. (*He reads the name on the front of the leaflet*) "The Meadows".
Albert Ha, that's a laugh for a start. "The Meadows". Have a good look at that picture on the front, Stanley. The grass has

been painted on. I tell you, there's more grass on this allotment than there is round the so-called bloody Meadows.

Lottie That's because it hadn't grown when they took the picture. I bet there's grass there now. Sally, you go past there every day. Is there grass there now?

Sally I'm saying nothing. I don't want to take sides on this one.

Dennis But you have to take sides, Sally. You've encouraged your grandad and you can see how it's affected your grandma.

Lottie I'm just frightened that if the people in charge get to know about him being a trouble-maker, they'll stop us getting a flat. I mean, they won't want his sort, will they? I mean, they'll be worried that he'll organise one of those sit-ins in the TV lounge if he can't watch *Grandstand*.

Stanley Who runs "The Meadows", Mrs Briggs?

Lottie The Council, I think.

Stanley (*quietly*) Oh dear.

Dennis Come on Lottie, it's time you were home. We're wasting our time here. Nobody could make that man see reason.

Albert Elizabeth might. I assume my daughter will be coming to see me sometime today.

Sally (*quietly*) Nice one, Grandad.

Dennis Yes, er ... well, she's awfully busy with her blanket squares for Upper Volta. And then of course, there's her, er ... trouble.

Albert Oh, we mustn't forget her trouble.

Dennis Look, I really do have to go. Try and think about what we've said, father-in-law. We have hopes and feelings too, you know. Make sure your grandma gets home all right, Sally. And tell your mother I'll be back from Huddersfield about six. I know it's only cold meat for tea, but she likes to know where I am.

Dennis exits

Sally Come on then, Grandma, better do as my father says. Here, I'll carry your bag for you.

Lottie Oh, I nearly forgot. (*She takes a packet of biscuits out of her bag, and gives them to Albert*) Here you are. I was going to make you some sandwiches but they wouldn't let me.

Albert (*slightly embarrassed by her kindess*) Trying to starve me out were they?

Lottie And I brought your cardigan in case the wind turns round. Now have you got a clean vest on?

Albert God, Lottie you sound just like my mother used to. Terrified I was going to get run over by a bus.

Stanley Do you know, mine was just the same. I grew up convinced that there was a phantom double-decker which only existed to mow down little boys with grubby underpants and holes in their socks.

Lottie It was if the police came and took you away. Elizabeth said they might.

Albert Look love, if the whole of the Special Branch came down here, they're hardly likely to strip me to my underwear before they arrest me.

Sally Come on, Grandma. And don't worry. Nobody's going to arrest him.

Stanley Oh, Mrs Briggs, you've forgotten your leaflet.

Lottie Oh you can keep it, Mr Fothergill, I've got several more at home. (*Quietly*) See if you can get *him* to read it.

Sally and Lottie exit

Stanley (*approaching Albert*) You ought to read it you know.

Albert Give it here then, I'll look at it sometime. Huh! Painted grass! Anyway, Stanley Fothergill, how are the angles looking? Are we any nearer a story?

Stanley No, Albert, sad to say we are not. To be perfectly frank, the most intriguing part of the whole day is your daughter's trouble.

Albert Oh that. She goes on about her trouble as much as he goes on about his promotion. I think it's what they call the change of life. Do you know, I'm sure they didn't have the change of life in my generation. If they did, I never heard about it.

Stanley I think it came in with the Common Market—like cholesterol and patio doors.

Albert And pre-menstrual tension. That's another one. *Woman's Realm* is full of pre-menstrual tension these days.

Stanley Ah no, I can speak with authority on pre-menstrual tension. My wife suffered with it every single day of our marriage.

Albert I didn't know you'd been married.

Stanley I don't like to talk about her.

Albert Why? Did she die?

Stanley Worse than that. She went to live in Cheshire.

Albert Well, I suppose somebody has to.

Stanley We weren't married all that long, though it seemed like it at the time, to both of us. It wasn't what you'd call an eventful marriage. We were polite, even cheerful on odd occasions, but nothing to put a spring in your step.

Albert So what happened?

Stanley Oh she started moaning because I had to work on Saturdays all through the summer. I tried to explain to her that most weddings don't happen on a wet Tuesday in November, but once she got a complaint lodged in her mind it took a lot of shifting. So I took her with me. After about three weeks it happened.

Albert What did?

Stanley She ran off with the wedding photographer. While he was lining up his family groups, she'd obviously been lining him up. They left. Went to live in Macclesfield. They're doing very well, I believe. Two kids and three photographic shops.

Albert I'm sorry, Stanley.

Stanley Funny looking little bloke he was too. Don't know what she saw in him. Mind you, I don't know what she saw in me either.

Albert I'm really sorry.

Stanley Do you know what really upset me? It was the only time in my working life that I ever got close to a good, scandalous story—and I couldn't use it.

Albert You've not had a particularly successful time out of life have you Stanley?

Stanley Oh, it's had its ups and downs, though I must admit I find it increasingly difficult to remember the ups.

Fiona Sinclair enters. She is dressed in a waxed cotton coat, long skirt and green tights

Fiona Is one of you gentlemen Mr Albert Briggs?

Stanley points across to Albert. Fiona strides enthusiastically across to him

Thank goodness you're still here Mr Briggs. I was afraid you might have changed your mind, or the whole thing might be a hoax. I can see now that I had no need to worry.

Albert And who might you be?

Fiona Forgive me, I was letting my enthusiasm run away with me. Fiona Sinclair, prospective parliamentary candidate for the Ecology Party.

Albert (*pointing to her green tights*) That's a very bad attack of greenfly on your legs. I should get them sprayed as soon as you can.

Fiona Mr Briggs, I think it's wonderful that a man of advanced years can retain his sense of humour at a time like this.

Albert At a time like what?

Fiona When the massed ranks of the establishment are bearing down on you trying to steal away your birthright.

Albert Massed ranks? I haven't seen any massed ranks, have you, Stanley?

Stanley No, I don't think so. The odd straggler, but no massed ranks. It's a good phrase though. (*He takes out his notebook*) Massed ranks of the ... er ... what was it again?

Fiona Establishment.

Stanley Thank you. Yes, I like that. How I can bring it into a wedding or funeral report, I don't quite know, but it's a very good phrase.

Fiona Are you a journalist?

Stanley I am, of sorts. Stanley Fothergill at your service, madam.

Fiona This is wonderful. Just what we need to get our message across to the great British public.

Albert Our message?

Fiona We in the Ecology Party believe ... shouldn't you be taking this down?

Albert Just a minute. I hate to interrupt your party political broadcast, but I'm not sure I like this *we* that's suddenly come into the conversation. This is my allotment and my argument. I'm not about to hand it over. What are you doing here anyway? I didn't invite you.

Fiona Ah, we have a mole in the council typing pool.

Stanley That could make quite a mess of the carpet.

Fiona No it's not that sort of mole. It's ... ah ... now you're teasing me.

Albert What is this Ecology Party anyway? Do you know anything about it, Stanley?

Stanley I think it's another thing that came in with the Common Market.

Fiona You may well mock, but the Ecology Party has a clear commitment to society. We exist to push back the barriers of bureaucratic interference in the natural environment.

Albert And how many of you are there?

Fiona In this area, six.

Albert By God, you'll have to push bloody hard with only six of you.

Fiona We've doubled our membership in less than a year.

Albert I can almost hear them trembling with fear in Westminster.

Stanley It occurs to me that if someone wanted to organise a flag day for the National Society for the Protection of the Inadequate, they could do a lot worse than start here.

Fiona Look, why are you being so cynical and hostile? Mr Briggs—the Ecology Party is on your side. We are with you all the way.

Albert And in a few weeks' time when I'm shovelling manure and digging it all over, will you be with me all the way then?

Fiona Yes, of course.

Albert You weren't the last time I dug it.

Fiona I didn't live here then. I've only recently moved into the town.

Stanley Where do you live, Miss Sinclair?

Fiona Over at Fenner's Lane.

Stanley Oh, those big new houses. There used to be fields down there. And a brook.

Albert I used to go looking for newts down there when I was a lad.

Fiona (*embarrassed*) Yes, well let's concentrate on the present shall we? What would you like me to do?

Albert I'd like you to go home love.

Fiona Oh no, I'm staying. Nothing would make me leave.

Ms Charlesworth and Councillor Hamshaw enter

Hamshaw Anyone here own a yellow Renault Five, registration number PMJ two-four-two Y?

Fiona Yes, I do. Why?

Hamshaw You're parked on double yellow lines and there's a traffic warden about to bust a gut with excitement.

Fiona Oh no, and my tax has run out.

Fiona exits

Hamshaw (*taking Ms Charlesworth aside*) Right Ms Charlesworth, which one's Briggs? The tatty geriatric or the vacant one with the crumpled suit and the carrier bag?

Ms Charlesworth That's Mr Fothergill. I think he's basically harmless. Mr Briggs, however, is an altogether tougher customer. Very cunning in a rather vulgar sort of way. I think it's in the breeding. You'll need to watch him.

Hamshaw Ms Charlesworth, I have dealt with rampant Trade Unions, I have dealt with sadistic VAT men, I have even on one occasion had to deal with a hysterical deputation from the Townswomen's Guild. Not a pretty sight, I can assure you. Compared to that lot, this will be like catching tiddlers. Now just stand there, watch, and admire.

Ms Charlesworth Certainly, Councillor Hamshaw. But don't be lulled into a false sense of security.

Hamshaw Ms Charlesworth, do I *look* like the sort of man to be lulled into a false sense of security?

Ms Charlesworth No, Councillor Hamshaw, I was merely going to point out ...

Hamshaw Well don't. Just leave this to me. (*He approaches Albert*) Now then Mr Briggs, I understand we're having a little local difficulty here.

Albert Are we?

Hamshaw I can see you're as surprised about it as I am. But I'm sure we can talk it through, man to man.

Albert Man to man eh? Is that why you've brought Ms Charlesworth along?

Ms Charlesworth (*moving forward*) Really, Councillor Hamshaw, I must protest.

Hamshaw Stay there, Ms Charlesworth. Now, Mr Briggs, we don't want any unpleasantness to Ms Charlesworth, do we? I mean, you've upset her once already today. Quite purple with rage she was when she got back to the planning department.

Ms Charlesworth Councillor Hamshaw, you promised. (*She again moves forward*)

Hamshaw Stay there.

Albert Wait a minute! Don't I know you?

Hamshaw That's quite possible. (*He begins to walk about, swelling with his own importance*) I have achieved something of a name in this town. Some folks know me as Councillor Hamshaw and other folks know me as the Mayor. (*To Ms Charlesworth*) You see Ms Charlesworth, we've hooked our fish. Just stay there and watch me land him.

Albert Piggy Hamshaw!

Hamshaw I beg your pardon.

Albert Piggy Hamshaw. You were in my class at Walker Street Elementary. Remember? That's what everyone called you. Piggy Hamshaw. You were the one who couldn't read and write. And you used to cry every playtime.

Hamshaw (*quickly moving to Ms Charlesworth*) I think perhaps you'd better go Ms Charlesworth.

Ms Charlesworth But you just told me to stay here, Councillor Hamshaw. Several times.

Hamshaw Yes, well I've just remembered something. Get back to the planning office and tell Simkins to have the JCB standing by at ten o'clock tomorrow morning. But tell him to check with me before it leaves the depot.

Ms Charlesworth Why, Councillor Hamshaw? Is this proving more difficult than you thought?

Hamshaw No, no. We'll soon have this sorted out. But you know, discretion is the better part of valour. Now off you go.

Ms Charlesworth exits

Albert You got rid of her in a hurry, didn't you?

Hamshaw I've found that when there's sensitive matters to be negotiated, it's best to get rid of the women. They tend to get sidetracked.

Albert Piggy Hamshaw! Well, I never!

Stanley (*writing in his notebook*) Did you call him Piggy because he looked like a pig, or because he was a messy eater?

Hamshaw Ah, you must be Fothergill, the funerals and weddings man.

Stanley That's right.

Hamshaw Well what are you doing here? I mean, statistically speaking, someone's bound to have died somewhere in this town, so shouldn't you be there?

Stanley No, I'm on holiday.

Hamshaw So what are you writing in your book for?

Stanley Habit. Whenever I spot a good story, I instinctively reach for my notebook. Go on Albert. You were telling me about our Mayor's schooldays.

Hamshaw Look, here's a tenner. Go and get yourself a pint.

Stanley I see. "Mayor In Bribery Attempt". This gets better all the time.

Hamshaw You wouldn't dare. I'd have you for libel.

Stanley Oh, I don't think so. "Piggy Hamshaw In Libel Suit". Wouldn't look very good in print would it. Besides, I've got no money, and *The Chronicle* wouldn't pay.

Albert Go on, settle out of court. Give him his tenner back.

Hamshaw snatches back his money, and tries manfully to appear calm

Hamshaw Now look here Mr Briggs, or can I call you Albert?

Albert No.

Hamshaw Now look here, Albert. We're both reasonable men.

Stanley Be careful, Albert. Whenever anyone says "we're both reasonable men" you can be sure that at least one of them isn't.

Hamshaw So just try to see it from my side. I've got a brand new council building over there, fitted out right down to the toilet rolls in the Gents, I've got a car park tarmacked and the white lines already painted on. I've got a road to get the cars in. But at the moment, they'll have to stay there because there's no way out.

Stanley That'll do wonders for productivity.

Hamshaw There's even a chance of getting Roy Hattersley to come and do the opening ceremony.

Albert Not *the* Roy Hattersley?

Hamshaw Well, you have to push the boat out sometimes. I mean the town deserves a treat. And you can help it get one just by moving off your allotment. It's not even as if we're stopping your gardening. There's another allotment waiting for you— now. You can take over this afternoon.

Albert Aye, about three miles away. I've got no car you know. I'd feel a right idiot getting on a twenty-seven bus with a spade and a fork and a barrowload of ripe manure. Besides, if I get a new allotment, I'd have to do things with it, just to keep up appearances.

Hamshaw Do you know, I despise people like you. You're just one of life's wreckers. You ruin everything people try to do, stand in the way of everything they try to achieve. I mean, I've done things with my life. Started with a lock-up garage, and look at me now. Biggest industrial clothing business in the

North of England. And now Mayor of this town. And why? Because I didn't let anyone stand in my way, or take away what was mine. Well, that council building's mine and I'm damned if I'll let you take away my little bit of glory. I'm a success, Briggs, and I'm going to stay a success. And who the hell are you to try and stop me?

Albert Me? Oh, I'm nobody. I don't own much and I've never amounted to much. I just worked down the pit for forty years digging out coal until some doctor found out that my lungs were breathing in nearly as much as I was digging out. They gave it some fancy name that I couldn't pronounce and waved me goodbye. Well since then the only pleasure I've had is sitting on this allotment watching the days go by. I reckon I've earned this allotment. And if I have, I've also earned the right to do what I choose with it. And if I choose to do sod all but grow grass and weeds, then fair enough. The world's had its money's worth out of me, and this is all I'm going to get in return. And by God, I'm going to hang on to it. And not even your council buildings and your tarmackcd exit roads and your Roy bloody Hattersleys will make me shift.

Hamshaw We'll see about that. (*He begins to exit*)

Albert Oh, Piggy. Just one question.

Hamshaw What?

Albert Did you ever learn to read and write?

Hamshaw I'll get you off that allotment Briggs. By tomorrow, that patch of land will be buried under eighteen inches of smooth, black, shiny tarmac.

Albert Over my dead body!

Hamshaw If necessary!

Hamshaw exits

There is a moment's silence

Stanley And I thought I was going to have a quiet, uncomplicated holiday.

Albert Well, Stanley, I hope you haven't been bored.

Stanley Definitely not bored. It's been like one of those medical programmes on the box, where they cut the body open and you see all the insides, exposed and quivering. It's not very pleasant to watch but it does have a certain morbid fascination. Anyway, it's time you went home. It's starting to get cold.

Albert No, I'm not going home. I'm staying here tonight. I wouldn't put it past those buggers to bring their machines in at dead of night.

Stanley Yes, and then put the rates up to pay for the overtime.

Albert Do me a favour, Stanley. Ring our Elizabeth and tell her I'm staying with you. Otherwise they'll only try to stop me. Six-nine-four-seven-one-two.

Stanley Just a minute, Albert. It's a golden rule of journalism—stay outside the story don't get involved.

Albert Please.

Stanley Oh, all right then, if you're sure you'll be all right. What was that number again?

Albert Six-nine-four-seven-one-two.

Stanley writes it down and prepares to leave

Stanley, what you said just now about staying outside the story. Does that mean you think we've got a story?

Stanley It's looking a bit more promising, but there's a long way to go yet. Still, who knows what tomorrow may bring?

Stanley exits

Albert sits down and tries to make himself comfortable. He shivers, gets up, notices the Union Jack on the shed. He takes it down and sits down again wrapping the flag round him. As he does so, we hear the sound of a telephone ringing. It is answered by the voice of Councillor Hamshaw

Hamshaw (*off*) Mayor's parlour. Hamshaw speaking ... Ah, Mr Simkins. What can I do you for? ... Yes that's right, Mr Simkins, ten o'clock ... No, Mr Simkins, Ms Charlesworth did not get the message wrong. Whatever else you may say about our Ms Charlesworth, she is not the sort of person to get messages wrong ... Don't worry about Briggs. One way or another, he'll be off that allotment by tomorrow. Oh just one thing Mr Simkins, did Ms Charlesworth say anything else to you when she got back? ... Are you sure ...? ... Nothing about schools or reading and writing? ... No, no reason, Mr Simkins. I just wondered, that's all ... Goodbye Mr Simkins.

During this speech Albert settles down and falls asleep, while the lights dim and then come up to denote the passage of time. Albert remains in his chair, not moving

Stanley enters, reading The Sun, *and still carrying his carrier bag.
He sits on the bench*

Stanley 'Morning, Albert. Glad to see you got a good night's
sleep. That's more than I did. Don't know why. Anyway, you
just carry on. Conserve your energy. I've got a feeling you might
need it later on. (*He begins to read* The Sun *with occasional
sounds of disgust and despair*) I don't know why I bothered to
buy this. "T.V. Comic in Sex Change Scandal". (*He turns pages*)
"My Night of Pleasure with the England World Cup Squad".
Hello, there's a bit of news here! (*He reads*) No, false alarm. I
tell you Albert, if World War Three started tomorrow, it
wouldn't make *The Sun*, unless the button was pressed by a
twenty-four-year-old model from Croydon with a large and
readily available cleavage.

Sally and Dennis enter arguing

Sally What do you mean, it's my fault?
Dennis You encouraged him in this. Well, I hope you're satisfied.
Perhaps now you'll start to behave with a bit more responsibi-
lity, instead of joining in with lies and deceit. (*He sees Stanley*)
And as for you, I'm going to report you to the Press Council.
Stanley What have I done?
Dennis I have just had a very interesting conversation with your
landlady. Charming woman. It seems you returned home alone
last night, and left the house alone this morning.
Stanley Oh.
Dennis Well, this has gone far enough. He's leaving. Now. Wake
him up, Sally.

Sally hesitates for a moment, then goes to Albert

He's leaving even if I have to put him over my shoulder and
carry him every inch of the way home. And if you want to make
something of that, well go ahead.
Sally Dad, I can't wake him.
Dennis What do you mean?
Sally I think he's dead.

*Dennis moves to the allotment and tries to find a pulse in Albert's
wrist and neck*

Dennis Sally, you stay here. I'll go and get an ambulance. (*He turns to Stanley*) You know, Mr Fothergill, you're priceless. You've been sitting here for God knows how long with a dead body, and you didn't even know.

Dennis exits

Stanley approaches the allotment very slowly and reluctantly. Sally sits in silence, holding Albert's hand. A sudden thought strikes Stanley and he rushes to his carrier bag, gets out his notebook and starts writing feverishly, occasionally looking up for inspiration

Stanley picks up his carrier bag and exits hurriedly

Sally Oh, Albert, you silly old bugger. You wanted the world to sit up and take notice. Well, you've done it now, haven't you? You've really done it now.

Stanley enters, walking very slowly

He looks across at Sally and Albert for a moment, then walks to the waste bin, tears pages out of his notebook, screws them up and throws them into the basket

CURTAIN

FURNITURE AND PROPERTY LIST

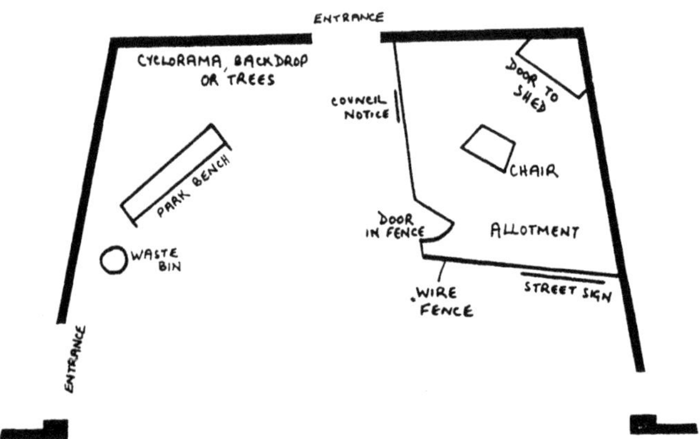

On stage: **Allotment area**
Grass
Assorted rubbish: broken tools, seed boxes etc
Garden chair
Shed or shed door
Other dressing as desired

Around allotment
Wire fence (sagging)
On fence: Council notice, street sign

Park bench
Wastepaper bin (full)

Personal: **Sally:** bag. *In it:* flask of tea, Union Jack, cheque book
Albert: pipe, Daily Mirror
Stanley: carrier bag. *In it:* newspaper, 2 packets of sandwiches.
  Diary. Notebook and pencil
Ms Charlesworth: clipboard. Plastic bag containing money
Lottie: bag. *In it:* leaflet, packet of biscuits, cardigan

CHARACTERS

Albert Briggs
Sally Parsons, his grand-daughter
Stanley Fothergill
Ms Charlesworth
Denis Parsons, Albert's son-in-law
Lottie Briggs, Albert's wife
Fiona Sinclair
Councillor Hamshaw

The scene is a street and allotment in a Northern town

Time—the present

LIGHTING PLOT

Exterior setting. No practical fittings required

To open: Black-out

Cue 1   **Hamshaw:** "If she's the one I think ..."   (Page 1)
Light gradually increases to daylight

Cue 2   **Hamshaw:** "Oh, just one thing Mr Simkins ..."   (Page 31)
Lights dim to denote passing of time, then up to daylight

EFFECTS PLOT

Cue 1   As Curtain rises   (Page 1)
Telephone rings

Cue 2   As **Albert** wraps Union Jack around himself   (Page 31)
Telephone rings

MADE AND PRINTED IN GREAT BRITAIN BY
LATIMER TREND & COMPANY LTD PLYMOUTH

MADE IN ENGLAND